Love Always, Jesus

MARIA PILLAY

Love Always, Jesus

Letters from the
Father-heart of God

Love Always, Jesus
Letters from the Father-heart of God
First Edition, First Impression 2021
ISBN: 978-1-77630-675-6

Published by:
Inspired Publishing
PO Box 82058 | Southdale | 2135 Johannesburg, South Africa
Email: info@inspiredpublishing.co.za | www.inspiredpublishing.co.za

TABLE OF CONTENTS

ACKNOWLEDGEMENTS

This book would not have been possible without the Lord. I truly believe every word was guided by the Holy Spirit as I sought Him.

To my Uncle Phillip Arjnan who always saw more in me that I could ever see. I will always strive to make you proud.

To my mother and grandmother who made me strong. I remember you with much love.

To the women in my family - Sandra, Sharon, Sejal, Jade, Rekha and Venoasha. Every day you teach me what it means to be a strong woman.

My best friend, Noelene Arjnan. You always see the best in me. Thank you for pushing me beyond my comfort zones. You are the Monica to my Rachel.

My girl squad - Mpho Raborife, Nikita Coetzee, Lameez Omarjee, Bombi Mavundza and Devereaux Morkel. Every girl needs friends like you.

And finally thank you to Darren August and his team for inspiring me to take this step.

FOREWORD

This book takes you on an emotional rollercoaster. You get to experience every emotion with the author - the sweet moments, the low ones as well as the peaks and plateaus.

It can't be easy to be this vulnerable as a writer, giving a reader special access into your most private conversations and thoughts - especially around the topic of abandonment. But boy, am I glad Maria Pillay has done it, because it moved me to tears and I know it will have the same effect on others.

This book is about grace in the true sense of the word and it was written from the heart of one of the most graceful people I have ever had the privilege of meeting during my own life journey. Anyone who gets the privilege of meeting Maria Pillay knows her heart, because she wears it on her sleeve. She is also a stern believer in the power of prayer and prays over everything and everyone that is important to her.

I am so glad she has worn her heart on her sleeve again through writing this book and is using her conversations with God to show us that, no matter what the circumstances on earth look like for us, we are never alone. Our Father is always with us and He's always got our back.

- Mpho Raborife
News24 Managing Editor

PSALM 27:10

"Though my father and mother forsake me, the LORD will receive me."

INTRODUCTION

When I first started working on this book, I had an entirely different idea of what it would be about. The one thing I was certain of was that I would write what the Father wanted me to write, even if it went in the opposite direction to what I had originally intended. And that's exactly what happened. I thought I would write a story about my life but it turned into a love letter from the Father. Some chapters were hard to write as the emotions were raw when I wrote them, but I know now that I needed to go through each emotion and find out for myself just how faithful the Father is. As I listened to Him and penned down my own thoughts and questions in response, I found such peace. When we were little girls, most of us kept journals. On these pages, we wrote down our dreams, our heartbreaks and our future plans. Some of us still journal while others may have decided, after too many crushed dreams, that there was just no point to this. Love Always, Jesus is a reminder that the Father is with us all the time, not only in the milestones or heartbreaking seasons of our life but also in the ordinary, everyday moments.

WHOSE DAUGHTER IS THIS?

As a child, I heard this question often. I would be playing outside and would hear the question posed to my grandmother when some distant relative or friend visited. And after she had answered, the usual response would be: "ahh, shame, poor child."

There was nothing extraordinary about my story. I was just a child born out of wedlock to a teenage mom. My dad left before I was born and when I was about three, my mom eloped with my stepdad, leaving me with my grandparents.

Adults sometimes assume that children, especially really young children, don't remember much of their childhood. As a result, they speak carelessly, assuming the child doesn't really understand, that they're too young to be feeling something real. We assume that they will get over it. We assume.

I remember the day my mother left. She let me wear one of my prettiest dresses. I remember her plaiting my hair. My grand-mother was out fetching firewood as we did not have electricity at that time and my grandfather was asleep. His health had taken a turn for the worse, so he slept a lot.

I also remember my mother packing her bags. A car pulled up and a man got out. "I'm taking your mother away", he said, laughing. I didn't think much of it. My mother then loaded her bags into his car, hugged me and left. I remember the tears in her eyes, I remember standing there for the longest time, watching the car pull away, until it was just a blur in the distance. I remember crying out for her.

Our neighbours suddenly appeared out of nowhere. There was a lady named Ruth who scooped me up in her arms and took me to her house.

She prayed over me and then made me some tea and gave me some Marie biscuits.

There were angry shouts when my grandmother got home. I heard my grandfather yelling: "She left the child. She left the child."

A year later, I attended my mother's wedding. She was all dressed up in her bridal attire and I ran after her, calling "Mummy!"

She turned around, looked at 4-year-old me and said: "Don't call me mummy." Years later, the adult me realised that she probably meant, "Don't call me now, I'm going to be busy with the wedding". But at that moment, all I heard was "I'm not your mummy". I never called her mummy ever again.

My grandparents raised me, and when I did visit my mother, I was the child that was spoken about in whispers. When my mom gave birth to my sisters and brother, they just assumed that I was their cousin, and I went along with it. You see, I learnt a long time ago, to make myself invisible, not to cause trouble for the adults. When my sisters would ask me who my mom was, I would tell them one of my aunts was my mom.

Who is your mother or who is your father? If people didn't see me, they wouldn't ask me questions. I wouldn't then have to deal with the feeling of dread when they asked: "Who's your father?" Sometimes I pretended not to hear the question, and other times I would just ignore the question and tell them who my grandfather was. Sometimes my answer was: "Oh, you don't know him". When what I actually meant to say was "I don't know him."

Sometimes I just stared at them blankly till they lost interest and focused their attention on something else.

It's very easy to grow up filled with resentment when you feel you've been abandoned. People mostly only associate abandonment with a child that's been left on a street corner or dropped off at an orphanage. They assume that if you were left with a family member, you were not really abandoned. At least there was someone taking care of you, they reason.

I watched my mother raise her children, while I stood on the outside, looking in. I remember being so angry with her that I would scream at her and throw her bags out when she came to visit me at my grandmother's house. But, as a child, you still are hopeful, you crave your mother's love.

As a teenager, I also remember wanting so desperately to feel loved by her that I would sometimes put my hands on her shoulders affectionately and she would brush my hands away. Every time she did that, a part of me just went to pieces.

Now, make no mistake, my mother was not a horrible woman. She was just a woman who found herself in a desperate predicament and she dealt with it the best she could.

Over the years I learnt to forgive my mother and our relationship healed. I always loved her, but I had to let go of the anger I felt. Even when my mother passed away, there were people at her funeral who didn't know who I was. They walked in, sympathised with my siblings and walked right past me. It was not their fault.

I gave my heart to the Lord at the age of 22. And that's when I discovered real love, the love of a Father.

That scripture in Hebrews 13:5 that says "I will never leave you nor forsake you" became so real to me. God really did know me before I was formed in my mother's womb. And even if she forgot, He didn't.

And yes, real life is not like the movies. There are times I wish I knew what it's like to have my mother dish up my food or pick out my clothes. I longed to know what it's like to have an earthly father.

I often asked the Lord why he didn't let me have a "normal life". Why did I not have the love of a mother and father? And He has always reminded me that He's always been there, even when I couldn't see it.

I have been asked many times: "Whose child, are you?" and for the longest time I dreaded that question. But now, I finally know WHOSE child I am. I know my Father and He has loved me with an everlasting love. His love is greater than any love I have ever known. He has taken every broken piece in me and made me whole again. I finally know whose child I am. I am my Father in heaven's daughter.

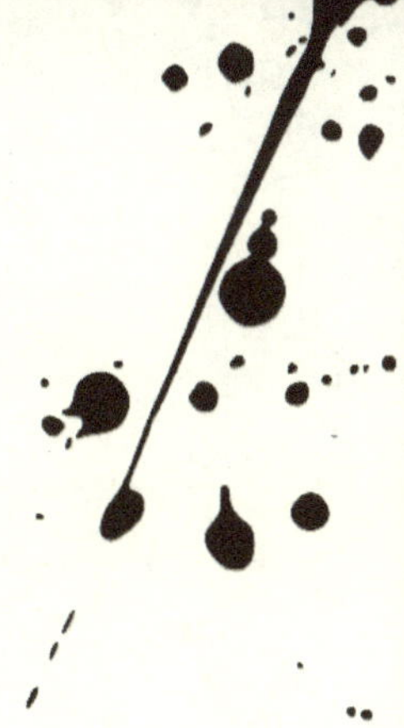

PART 1

WINTER'S CHILD

PSALM 74:17

"It was You who set all the boundaries of the earth; You made both summer and winter."

Dear Daughter,

It's almost time for you to leave the womb. Any day now you will meet your mother. She's quite anxious. She's excited to meet you but she's also afraid. You see, she feels alone in this. She's young and unmarried. She knows she's disappointed her family. She knows people are whispering about her. Your father didn't stick around, so she feels alone and heartbroken. She's unsure of what's going to happen next. But she does love you.

I look at you in the womb, so fearfully and wonderfully made. I carefully wove you together. You are perfectly formed. Always remember, even before you were formed in your mother's womb, I knew you. I have loved you with an everlasting love. No matter what life brings your way, I will be here. I have such great plans for you. When you begin to see yourself through My eyes, you will realise just how special you are to me. In this world you will have trouble. But take heart! I have overcome the world.

JEREMIAH 1:5

"Before I formed you in the womb I knew you,
before you were born, I set you apart."

Dear Daughter,

Today was quite an adventure for you. You left the comfort of the womb and entered screaming into a world you haven't yet adjusted to.

There are bright lights and all these strange people staring at you, turning you upside down, trying to get you to breath and then to cry. It's all so confusing.

Then they handed you to her.

You're seeing her face for the first time, but you know the sound of her voice. She also looked at you differently, with so much love. You felt safe when you saw her. She held you gently. She looked a bit unsure, maybe a bit terrified, but there was something about her that made you feel so connected to her. Your journey together will not always be easy but through it, you will find your strength and your purpose. I see you're sleepy now. I will let you be. But I will watch over you. You are my precious child. I know the plans I have for you.

PSALM 139:13-14

"For you formed my inward parts; you knitted me together in my mother's womb. I praise you, for I am fearfully and wonderfully made. Wonderful are your works; my soul knows it very well."

Dear Daughter,

So much has changed in the last few years. Oh, how you've grown. You love talking to yourself and creating a make believe world. You are now 3-years-old and as I watch you play in the garden, I see your sadness. Your mother moved away today. She will be getting married soon and you will be raised by your grandparents. I saw the tears you cried when she drove away with the man who will become your stepdad. You didn't want to cry, you tried to be a big girl, but the tears wouldn't stop rolling. You felt scared and alone. You looked so confused, yet somehow you tried to be brave. You told yourself that she will come back but, even if she didn't, you would be strong.

She also looked so heartbroken as she packed her bags. You didn't know why at the time. You wonder how could she still leave you if it made her so sad to do so? You do not know my Name yet, precious daughter. But I know you. I was there when you cried out for your mother. Do you remember the women from the neighbourhood who gathered around and comforted you? I sent them. And when they prayed over you, I was there, holding you. Could you sense my presence? You may not yet understand the reasons why adults make the decisions they do but one day you will. The heartache you feel today will equip you to comfort someone else. It's never my will to cause you pain. I love you so much. My heart hurts when you hurt. Child of Mine, I will walk with you every step of the way.

ISAIAH 49:15

"Can a woman forget her nursing child and have no compassion on the son of her womb? Even these may forget, but I will not forget you."

Dear Father,

PSALM 61:2

"From the end of the earth, I call to You when my heart is faint.
Lead me to the rock that is higher than I."

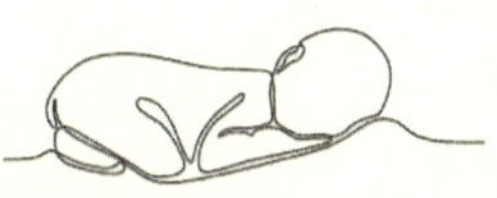

Dear Daughter,

Your mother came to visit today. She baked you a cake for your 13th birthday. You were excited to see her, but you have adjusted to life without her. She visits you every month and you wait for her visits - but deep down you're angry at her. She has other children now. You love spending time with them. They love you too, but they think you're their cousin, and you go along with it. I see the heartache in your eyes as you watch your mother with them. You're jealous of the life they have with her, but you will not let anyone see your pain. You wish you could just scream at your mother, ask her why she left you behind, tell her she's a horrible person. But you don't. Instead, you put a smile on your face and pretend it doesn't hurt. You pretend not to hear the whispers when adults discuss "the child that she left behind." You wish adults would realise that you hear them and that their conversations about you cause you such pain. But you're invisible to them, well you've decided to make yourself invisible. Oh child, do not let yourself become bitter. Forgive them. Forgive HER. Your mother is my daughter too. I love her just as much as I love you. You do not know this, but she has spent many nights wrestling with her decisions and weeping for the child she had to leave behind. She puts a smile on her face, but she also has a great emptiness deep within. But while she's gone, I will be your comfort. I am He who watches over you.

ISAIAH 66:13

"As a mother comforts her child, so will I comfort you."

Dear Father,

MATTHEW 27:46

"About the ninth hour Jesus cried out with a loud voice, saying, "Eli, Eli, lama sabachthani?" that is, "My God, My God, why have You forsaken Me?"

Dear Daughter,

Your best friend invited you to church today. It was so good to see you there. You were all dressed up in your Sunday best. You even carried a little bible that your friend lent you. I saw you walk into that little church building, a little nervous and unsure but also excited. I want you to know I am always with you no matter where you are. You have heard my Name so many times, so I know you are curious. I've seen you page through your friend's Bible. The stories intrigue you. I heard you singing along. "Wonderful, wonderful, Jesus is to me." The first worship song you ever sang. My heart leapt when I heard you say my Name for the very first time.

But you're also distracted by the things of this world. You're in high school now and you fell in love for the first time, so your attention is elsewhere. But I am patient. I will wait for you. I will watch over you. I will never leave you. Through every heartbreak, every lesson learnt, every new chapter, I will be here, watching from a distance. And when you call my Name, I will be there in a heartbeat.

PSALM 121:5-8

"The LORD watches over you—
the LORD is your shade at your right hand;
the sun will not harm you by day, nor the moon by
night. The LORD will keep you from all harm—
he will watch over your life; the LORD will watch over your coming
and going both now and forevermore."

Dear Father,

PSALM 42:2

"My soul thirsts for God, for the living God; When shall I come and appear before God?"

Dear Daughter,

Your heart was dealt a major blow today. You let someone into your life that you thought would love you and care for you. But he taught you what it means to be afraid of another human being. He told you he loved you and then he broke you down so that you didn't recognize yourself anymore. He was someone you wanted to spend the rest of your life with but now you feel caged and afraid. You wish you had seen the red flags. You wonder if this is going to be your life. You are mad at yourself too because you never thought you would be in a situation like this. You had tried so hard to always make wise decisions. You tried so hard not to make the same mistakes your mother did. My child, there will be many times in your life that you may mistake certain actions as love when it's not. This world has taken the meaning of love and distorted it. But I am here to tell you I am love. When I say I love you, it is the most truthful thing you will ever hear. My love is patient, my love is kind, it does not envy, it does not boast. It does not dishonour others, it is not self-seeking, it is not easily angered, it keeps no record of wrongs.

My Love does not delight in evil but rejoices with the truth. It always protects, always trusts, always hopes, always perseveres.

Now as you lie in bed, you find yourself crying out to Me, the God you had heard about in your childhood. You remembered how your friends would speak about Me. You wondered if I heard you, if I was even real. Do I even know your name? I want you to know that I am here. Especially when you feel alone and afraid, I am here. I will never leave you nor forsake you.

PSALM 18:6

"In my distress I called to the LORD;
I cried to my God for help.
From his temple he heard my voice;
my cry came before him, into his ears."

Dear Father,

PSALM 34:18

"The LORD is close to the broken hearted and saves those who are crushed in spirit."

Dear Daughter,

Love!

There will be moments in your life when you will find it very easy to show love and then there are moments when it will take everything in you just to even muster up a fake smile.

But precious one, remember love is patient, love is kind, it is not easily angered. No, these are not just pretty words we recite at a wedding ceremony.

These are words that need to be put into action.

It's so easy to judge someone when we don't know the road they've walked. Think of the time when you needed someone to show you a little kindness. Do you remember how much that meant to you? Now show that same kindness to someone else. That woman that pushed past you at the supermarket. You thought she was being rude, but she was in a hurry to get back home to see to her sick child. She hadn't slept in days, and she had forgotten to get bread to make her teenager a sandwich to take to school. Of course, you didn't know that. How could you? That's why I say, be kind, show love. You don't know who needs it today.

1 CORINTHIANS 13: 4-6

"Love is patient, love is kind. It does not envy, it doesnot boast, it is not proud. It is not rude, it is not selfseeking, it is not easily angered, it keeps no record of wrongs. Love does not delight in evil but rejoices with the truth."

Dear Father,

MATTHEW 18: 12

"What do you think? If a man has a hundred sheep, and one of them gets lost, will he not leave the ninety-nine on the mountain and go in search of the one that is lost?"

PART 2

SPRING IN HER STEP

SONG OF SONGS 2:11-13

"See! The winter is past; the rains are over and gone. Flowers appear on the earth; the season of singing has come; the cooing of doves is heard in our land. The fig tree forms its early fruit; the blossoming vines spread their fragrance. Arise, come, my darling; my beautiful one, come with me."

Dear Daughter,

We're starting afresh. My heart soared when I heard you invite me into your heart for the first time. All of heaven rejoiced. You are so loved, dear daughter. I know you have spent years feeling rejected and abandoned. And now as you take this step to start over, I know you are overwhelmed but as you read my Word, you will get to know my heart. I love you so much that I sent my son to die for you. I did not send Him into the world to condemn the world, but in order that the world might be saved through Him. Don't stay in a place of brokenness, my child. You are so precious to me. I know every strand of hair on your head. Your name is engraved on the palm of My Hand.

Oh, you are so loved. Daughter, you may be broken and bruised. But I am your Healer. I will bind up your wounds. I will set your feet upon the rock. The future may look scary and uncertain to you right now, but I've got this. I am your shelter from the storm. I will walk this journey with you. Oh, my child, if only you could see the things, I have planned for you. I will never harm you. I died for you. There is no greater love than that. Put your hand in Mine and let us walk this road together.

PSALM 147: 3

"He heals the broken hearted and binds up their wounds."

Dear Father,

ISAIAH 43:18-19

"Remember not the former things, nor consider the things of old. Behold, I am doing a new thing; now it springs forth, do you not perceive it? I will make a way in the wilderness and rivers in the desert."

Dear Daughter,

Let's take a walk together. I can see that you're having a tough day. You've been so quiet lately. Even though you have not said a word, I know what you're going through. You feel so inadequate, so unworthy. Fear not for I am here. The voices that you're listening to may tell you otherwise, but don't believe them. Oh, how I love you, you are so precious to Me. At times you feel so forgotten but trust Me, you are not. Yes, there will be hard days, but like different seasons, they will not last forever. You will laugh again, precious daughter. You will have peace again.

Doors are opening for you, but you feel so intimidated. You worry that you're not educated enough or not qualified enough. I will make a way where there seems to be no way. I have put so much in you and yet you have moments when you feel like such an imposter. Take heart, my child. Have I not told you that your gift will make room for you and bring you before great men? Just hold on to Me. You will not be brought to shame.

PROVERBS 31:25

"Strength and dignity are her clothing,
And she smiles at the future."

Dear Father,

ROMANS 8:28

"And we know that for those who love God all things work together for good, for those who are called according to his purpose."

Dear Daughter,

You passed your driving test today. You were so nervous but look, you did it! Remember when you thought that you would never be able to drive. You were always so scared of all the things that could go wrong. And yet, here you are. You did it. When you have moments in your life where you may feel inadequate, always remember that I have put so much in you. I have equipped you with everything you need. You make your Father's Heart swell with joy. I am so proud of you, child. I know it's been a tough few years. You have had to learn some hard lessons along the way, but you also found out how much you were capable of. You are not some discarded person that no one wants. Your birth may have been unplanned, but you are not a mistake. Not to Me. I have a plan and a purpose for your life. My Spirit dwells in you. When you need wisdom, ask. When it's direction you seek, I'm here to guide you. I will order your steps. Seek me and you will find me.

PSALM 37: 3-4

"3 Trust in the LORD and do good; dwell in the land and enjoy safe pasture. 4 Take delight in the LORD, and he will give you the desires of your heart."

Dear Father,

LUKE 1:47

"And my spirit has rejoiced in God my Saviour"

Dear Daughter,

You make me smile. Have I told you how much I love your childlike faith? Never lose that. Look at how far you've come. I saw you rejoice over some good news that you received today. I just wanted to pick you up in my arms and swing you around. After all, you are my little girl. This is the beginning of great things to come. The road will not always be easy, but you will never be alone. I will go through the good days and the difficult days with you. Even when you feel far away from me, I want you to know that I am always with you. I am your hiding place. Along this road, you may find others like you.

Those who are longing for acceptance, longing for love. As you grow in Me and my Word becomes rooted in you, I want you to become the friend that someone needs. Be the person who offers words of encouragement to a colleague who is having a bad day. Sow seeds of love wherever you go. Be a lighthouse to those who can't see the way out. Be an atmosphere changer!

ROMANS 8: 37-39

"No, in all these things we are more than conquerors through him who loved us. For I am convinced that neither death nor life, neither angels nor demons, neither the present nor the future, nor any powers, neither height nor depth, nor anything else in all creation, will be able to separate us from the love of God that is in Christ Jesus our Lord."

Dear Father,

PSALM 121: 1-2

"I will lift up mine eyes unto the hills, from whence cometh my help. My help cometh from the LORD, which made heaven and earth."

Dear Daughter,

It's Father's Day. I know you've never known what it's like to have an earthly father and I've heard you say it doesn't bother you. And yes, for the most part, I know it doesn't. But there are days when it does. You can hide it from the rest of the world, but you can't hide it from me. I've seen the look of longing on your face when you see your friends being hugged by their dads.

When you have car problems, I know you wish you could pick up the phone and say: "Dad, my car broke down, please come help me."

You have men in your life who have played the role of father but it's not quite the same, is it? You have often wondered why your father did not want you. You have imagined the questions you would ask if you ever met him. You wonder if your life would have been different if your father had stuck around. As you prayed tonight, you asked me for a hug. You wanted to feel the hug of a father. I was right there in that room with you. As you slept, I held you. Did you feel my Presence?

2 CORINTHIANS 6:18

"And, I will be a Father to you, and you will be my sons and daughters, says the Lord Almighty."

Dear Father,

PSALM 68:5-6

"[5] A father to the fatherless, a defender of widows, is God in his holy dwelling. [6] God sets the lonely in families, he leads out the prisoners with singing; but the rebellious live in a sun-scorched land."

Dear Daughter,

Forgive.

I love that you can be yourself when you talk to me. After all, there's nothing about you that I don't already know. Precious child, there's always going to be people in your life who will disappoint you or even betray you. Even I wasn't exempt from that. Remember Judas? But no matter what, always forgive. We will all be faced with people we need to forgive. No one is exempt. Yes, I know it's not always easy and yes, you may feel that they are not deserving of your forgiveness - and you may be right, but it's something you need to do. I was betrayed, beaten, mocked and hung on a cross but I forgave. I had to, so that you could be free.

Unforgiveness keeps you in a prison. The prison bars and keys may be invisible but they're there. It keeps you from moving forward. So, take some time. Write down their names if you have to and let them go. I will be with you every step of the way.

MATTHEW 6:14

"For if you forgive other people when they sin against you, your heavenly Father will also forgive you."

Dear Father,

2 CORINTHIANS 4:8-9

"We are afflicted in every way, but not crushed; perplexed, but not driven to despair; persecuted, but not forsaken; struck down, but not destroyed;"

Dear Daughter,

It's so easy to feel invisible in a world that only seems to notice the perceived perfect body shape or the pretty smile. But daughter, you so are much more than the number of Instagram or Facebook likes.

Remember when you were a little girl you would twirl around in front of the mirror. You loved how you smiled, and you loved your long, black hair. Then as you grew and started listening to the voices of those around, you started noticing your flaws in the things you once loved. Do not be deceived by this world, my child. The world's idea of beauty and Mine are polar opposites.

You are the apple of My eye. You are altogether beautiful, my darling; there is no flaw in you.

I see you look at yourself in the mirror just to point out your flaws. "My nose is too big. I wish I had a better smile. If only I were thinner." The list is endless.

You may feel invisible or forgotten right now but I'm here to tell you that I see you. I am El-Roi – the God who sees you. You can never be forgotten.

ISAIAH 49:15-16

"I will never forget you. See, upon the palms of my hand I have written your name."

Dear Father,

PSALM 139:14

"I praise you because I am fearfully and wonderfully made; your works are wonderful; I know that full well."

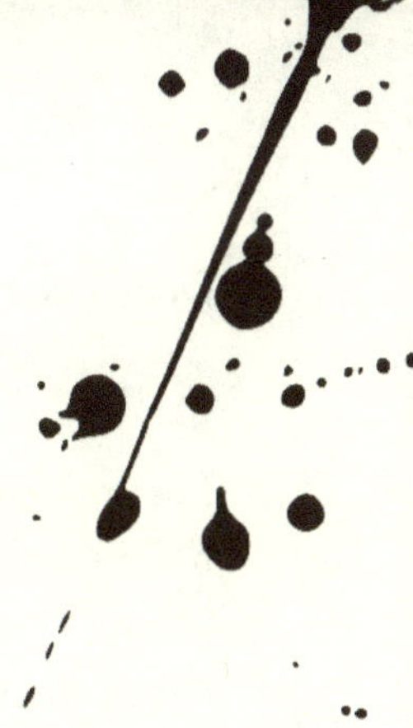

PART 3

SUMMER RAINS

PROVERBS 30:25

"Ants are creatures of little strength, yet they store up their food in the summer;"

Dear Daughter,

For so long you have longed for peace. You've longed for joy, and you have tried to find it in so many places and material things. Child, no amount of money, fancy cars or shopping trips will ever give you the peace or the joy that you seek. It may bring you happiness for a while but soon you will find yourself looking for the next high. I am your peace. My peace is not short lived. My peace will carry you through every season. You may not escape a season, but my peace will carry you through it. In the midst of turmoil, I am your refuge.

When the future seems uncertain, I am the One who goes before you to make the crooked paths straight. My peace does not only come when there's absence of trouble. My peace sustains you while you are waiting. My peace carries you when nothing else makes sense. Draw near to Me.

When you're going through a crisis, I know it seems natural to call up your closest friend or family member to tell them your troubles and hope they can offer solace. But the truth is, at times the most people can do is offer a sympathetic ear and hope for the best. There will also be people who will add to the turmoil so be so careful about who you share your trouble with. It's not their fault. There's only so much that they can do. But I know your end from your beginning. Come unto me when you are weary and heavy laden, and I will give you rest.

JOHN 14:27

"Peace I leave with you; my peace I give you. I do not give to you as the world gives. Do not let your hearts be troubled and do not be afraid."

Dear Father,

PSALM 4:8

"In peace I will lie down and sleep, for you alone, LORD, make me dwell in safety"

Dear Daughter,

You received a telephone call that changed your life. The voice at the other end told you that your mother had passed away. You didn't hear much after that.

I see you trying so hard to be strong. You tell yourself there's so much to be done so you cannot cry. You have to be strong for everyone else. You think of all the things you wanted to say to her, but you didn't. You wish you had stayed longer on the phone the last time you spoke to her. You thought you had more time.

I see you drowning in your tears, daughter. I held you as you lay on the floor, broken. You feel alone, but I am here. I am your shelter from the storm. You think I don't understand your pain. But I do. I watched my Son die a horrific death for sins He did not commit. There's no pain that you feel that I cannot resonate with. But, my precious child, it shall be well with your soul. Trust me.

JOHN 11:33

"When Jesus saw her weeping, and the Jews who had come along with her also weeping, he was deeply moved in spirit and troubled."

Dear Father,

2 THESSALONIANS 3:16.

"Now may the Lord of peace himself give you peace at all times and in every way. The Lord be with all of you."

Dear Daughter,

Let not your heart be troubled. The odds may be stacked against you but remember your Father goes before you and makes the crooked paths straight. Though the fires are raging around you, you are not in it by yourself. I will go before you and prepare a table for you in the presence of your enemies. My mercy will speak for you in rooms where your name is being mentioned. It doesn't matter what the situation looks like right now. I've got this. You may find yourself in a situation where you feel the whole world is against you. You may feel like the underdog, but I am your strong tower. I am the One who will fight your battles when you are unfairly accused. As I was with Shadrach, Meshach, and Abednego in the fire, so I will be with you. This too shall pass.

ISAIAH 43

"Fear not. I have redeemed you; I have summoned you by name; you are mine. When you pass through the waters, I will be with you; and when you pass through the rivers they will not sweep over you. When you walk through the fire, you will not be burned; the flames will not set you ablaze. For I am the LORD your God, the Holy One of Israel, your Saviour;"

Dear Father,

ZEPHANIAH 3:17

"The Lord your God is in your midst, a mighty one who will save; he will rejoice over you with gladness; he will quiet you by his love; he will exult over you with loud singing."

Dear Daughter,

Let's go on a lunch date today. You pick the place, and I will provide the company. There's so much I want to share with you. I know your day is busy so all I'm asking for is an hour. No distractions, no cell phones. Just you and I. Tell me about your day. What's on your mind today? If you don't want to talk, we can just walk together quietly. There are no awkward silences with me.

Besides, I know what you're thinking even when you don't say a word. See! I'm good company. Come away with me. For I know the plans I have for you, plans to prosper you and not to harm you, plans to give you hope and a future.

REVELATION 3: 20

"Here I am! I stand at the door and knock. If anyone hears my voice and opens the door, I will come in and eat with that person, and they with me."

Dear Father,

PHILIPPIANS 4:19

"And my God will supply every need of yours according to his riches in glory in Christ Jesus."

Dear Daughter,

My precious child, we need to talk about some of the conversations that you have been having. You say you love me and yet you spit out such unkind words about your fellow brothers and sisters. I know you think its harmless because you're not saying it to their faces. But words have power. Words are seeds. Seeds take root. What are you planting? What help are you to your sister or brother if you're discussing their weaknesses with someone else?

If you are going to discuss another person's weakness, do so with me. It does not matter what they did to hurt you. Bring it to me.

Remember the battle is mine. My child, do not regard lightly my discipline, nor be weary when I reprove you. For I discipline the one I love.

And if you have to speak about another, speak life.

JAMES 3: 9-12

"With the tongue we praise our Lord and Father, and with it we curse human beings, who have been made in God's likeness. Out of the same mouth come praise and cursing. My brothers and sisters, this should not be. Can both fresh water and saltwater flow from the same spring? My brothers and sisters, can a fig tree bear olive, or a grapevine bear fig? Neither can a salt spring produce fresh water."

Dear Father,

EPHESIANS 4:29

"Let no corrupting talk come out of your mouths, but only such as is good for building up, as fits the occasion, that it may give grace to those who hear."

Dear Daughter,

Hurt is something that you cannot escape. It's going to happen. The stinging part is that it will often come from places you did not expect. The very ones you hold closest to your heart may sometimes cause the biggest blow – it may be unintentional at times. But it will happen. Even I didn't escape betrayal. Judas ate with me, walked with me, laughed with me, sat at the table with me, broke bread with me. Peter denied me. But don't dwell in your place of hurt so long that it becomes your crutch. Don't spend so much time nursing that wound that it becomes your dwelling place.

Forgive. Let go. Yes, the words spat out at you broke your heart. It caused you to question who you are, but hurtful words do not define you. When you stay offended, bitterness takes root. And bitterness in itself is a prison. Bitterness leads to unforgiveness and causes separation.

No matter what was said to you, remember you are who I say you are. My Word says that you are loved, you are not useless, you have a Father who loves you. You are not abandoned. Rise up! Wash the tears off your face and rejoice. You are blessed and greatly favoured. You will no longer remember the shame of your youth. Even if those around you reject you, I never will. I will never leave you nor forsake you. You are my precious child.

PSALM 55:12-14

"For it is not an enemy who reproaches me, Then I could bear it; Nor is it one who hates me who has exalted himself against me, Then I could hide myself from him.
But it is you, a man my equal,
My companion and my familiar friend;
We who had sweet fellowship together
Walked in the house of God in the throng."

Dear Father,

LEVITICUS 19:18

"Thou shalt not avenge, nor bear any grudge against the children of thy people, but thou shalt love thy neighbour as thyself: I am the LORD."

Dear Daughter,

It's been a while since we've chatted. You've made some choices you're not proud of. I know there are days when you want to speak to Me, but you're so riddled with guilt that you stay away from Me. My precious child, when I told you that nothing can separate you from My love, I meant it. Yes, I'm not pleased with what has happened. I wish you hadn't done some of the things you did but I'm still here, waiting. Stop running away from Me. I have loved you with an everlasting love. You are never too far gone. I long to sit with you again and talk like we used to. I love listening to you worship. Remember when you could not wait to tell others about Me? It's still in you. I hear you asking for forgiveness for the same thing over and over again. I have forgiven you. My mercies are new every morning and new every day. Stop punishing yourself. Like the prodigal son was welcomed home by his father, I am here waiting to welcome you back. I can see you in the distance.

Don't stop. Keep walking towards me. You are My child.

ISAIAH 54: 7-10

"For a brief moment I abandoned you,
but with deep compassion I will bring you back.
In a surge of anger
I hid my face from you for a moment,
but with everlasting kindness
I will have compassion on you,"
says the LORD your Redeemer.
To me this is like the days of Noah,
when I swore that the waters of Noah would never
again cover the earth.
So now I have sworn not to be angry with you,
never to rebuke you again.
Though the mountains be shaken
and the hills be removed,
yet my unfailing love for you will not be shaken
nor my covenant of peace be removed,"
says the LORD, who has compassion on you."

Dear Father,

PSALM 36:7

"How precious is Your lovingkindness, O God. And the children of men take refuge in the shadow of Your wings."

PART 4

AUTUMN HOPES

ISAIAH 40:8

"The grass withers, the flower fades, but the word of our God will stand forever."

Dear Daughter,

When you were little, you fell off a tree and scraped your knee. Do you remember that day? Of course, you do – you have a scar that's a constant reminder. You wear it proudly like a badge of honour. Over the years I've heard you tell people that story with a big smile on your face. Yet, there are other scars that you bear that you don't show others. Those deep yet unseen wounds that stop you in your tracks and keep you from reaching your potential. Who told you that you were weak? I have armed you with strength and I will make your way perfect. Your parents may have abandoned you, but I haven't. I have adopted you into my own family and it has given Me great pleasure to do this. Someone told you that you're hopeless. Do not listen to them. For I know the plans I have for you, plans for welfare, and not for evil, to give you a future and a hope"

ESTHER 4:14

"My child, you are not purposeless. Perhaps this is the moment for which you've been created."

Dear Father,

ISAIAH 54:8

"In an outburst of anger, I hid My face from you for a moment, but with everlasting lovingkindness I will have compassion on you," Says the Lord your Redeemer"

Dear Daughter,

Wait!

They that wait upon the Lord shall renew their strength. They shall mount up with wings as eagles. They shall run and not faint. I know it's very tempting to rush ahead with certain things but wait on Me.

You may feel as if life is passing you by. Your friends are buying houses, planning weddings, travelling to exotic destinations. And you feel stuck. And yet still I say, wait!
And while you're waiting, praise Me.

While you're waiting, trust Me. While you're waiting, tell others about Me. It's not My will for you to be unhappy. I am your Father who adores you. I want to give you good things, things that will not just make you smile for a little while, but things that will fill your heart with joy. Don't settle for what is convenient. Wait, I have so much more for you. Trust Me. Have I ever let you down?

Remember, the steps of the righteous are ordered by the Lord.

PSALM 130:5

"I wait for the LORD, my whole being waits,
and in his word I put my hope."

Dear Father,

PROVERBS 18:21

"Death and life are in the power of the tongue, and those who love it will eat its fruits."

Dear Daughter,

When you were a little girl, you dreamt of having a family of your own. You pictured kids running around, filling your home with laughter. But life hasn't quite panned out that way. You wonder if this is some sort of punishment. You watch your friends with their kids, and you are still waiting. When will it be your turn? Will it ever be your turn? You've fasted and prayed. You've even begged Me to answer. Then you resigned yourself to your fate and told yourself to make the most of your situation.

But daughter, this is not a punishment. I have so much in store for you. I am the One who orders your steps. When the time is right, I will make it happen. I heard Hannah as she stood in the temple, pouring out her heart. Sarah laughed, and yet before long she was nursing Isaac. Elizabeth was past childbearing age, but I showed her favour. Is there anything too hard for Me?

In the meantime, I need you to trust me. I am your Father. I will never cause you harm.

ISAIAH 54

"Sing, barren woman, you who never bore a child;
burst into song, shout for joy, you who were never in labour;
because more are the children of the
desolate woman than of her who has a husband,"
says the LORD."

Dear Father,

PSALM 13: 1

"How long, LORD? Will you forget me forever? How long will you hide your face from me?"

Dear Daughter,

All it takes is one cry to reach My heart. I see you. I am El-Roi, the God who sees.

You may be lying in a crumpled heap right now, your heart broken, your self-confidence destroyed. I see you. You are not forgotten. You are not overlooked. I will make a way out. Arise Daughter. Rise from the dust, O Jerusalem. Sit in a place of honour. Remove the chains of slavery from your neck, O captive daughter of Zion.

No number of bad choices can separate you from my love. I stand at the door waiting. All you need to do is let Me in.

Weeping may endure for a night, but joy comes in the morning. Arise daughter. God's not done with you.

You are not forgotten. Have I not told you that your name is engraved in the palm of My hand? You may have been abandoned, rejected, pushed aside but I have not forgotten you. You are not a mistake. Arise! Stop hiding your light. You were made for a purpose. Yes, you may have scars, and so did I. When you look at my nail scarred hand it's a reminder of just how much I love you.

ISAIAH 54:4

"Do not be afraid; you will not be put to shame.
Do not fear disgrace; you will not be humiliated.
You will forget the shame of your youth
and remember no more the reproach of your
widowhood."

Dear Father,

SONG OF SOLOMON 2:11-12

"[11] For, lo, the winter is past, the rain is over and gone; [12] The flowers appear on the earth; the time of the singing of birds is come, and the voice of the turtle is heard in our land;"

Dear Daughter,

Let us go to that secret place, where it's just you and Me.

That place where you pour out your heart and when I pour into you.

When you dwell with Me in the secret place, your life will never be the same again. In this place you will know My Heart. Once you know My Heart; your heart will never be the same again. The things of this world will no longer hold the same pull over your life again. When you dwell in the secret place your life will begin to reflect Me.

You will no longer need to beg and plead with Me to change you because when you dwell in My Presence, it is impossible to leave the same way you came in. The key is to dwell, not just to pop in. Most people treat my presence like a drive through, they order what they need and leave. They will not step out of their comfort zones and allow me to really move in their lives. When you allow yourself to be drenched in the fragrance of My Presence, your life will never be the same again. It will show when you enter other rooms. My Presence will go before you. My mercy will speak for you.

PSALM 91: 1-2

"Whoever dwells in the shelter of the Most High will rest in the shadow of the Almighty.[a] I will say of the LORD, "He is my refuge and my fortress, my God, in whom I trust."

Dear Father,

HEBREWS 4:16

"Let us then approach God's throne of grace with confidence, so that we may receive mercy and find grace to help us in our time of need."

Dear Daughter,

Dream again.

There was a time when you had such big dreams. You wanted to start that company, write that book or record that album. But life happened and it stopped you in your tracks. You put your dreams on the back burner and just tried to make it through each day. Or maybe you took the first step, and you were rejected.

Someone told you that you were not good enough, so you gave up. Someone hurt you or told you your dreams were not valid. Even Joseph's brothers couldn't handle his dreams.

Daughter it is time to get up. All is not lost. It's never too late to start again. Some of the most successful people have had their ideas rejected many many times but the key is not to give up. You may have to go back to the drawing board, learn a few new skills, try things a little differently this time but don't let that dream die.

ISAIAH 43:18-19

"Do not remember the former things, nor consider the things of old. Behold, I will do a new thing, now it shall spring forth; Shall you not know it? I will even make a road in the wilderness and rivers in the desert."

Dear Father,

JEREMIAH 17:14

"Heal me O LORD, and I will be healed; save me and I will be saved, for you are the one I praise."

Dear Daughter,

This year has certainly not been what you expected. You started out with such great plans. Then one day while flipping channels you came across a story on the news about a virus that was killing people. It caught your interest for a few moments and then you moved on. After all, it was all happening in another country, far away from you.

And then a few weeks later, that virus suddenly wasn't so far away. It was suddenly in your hometown. The dead were no longer just numbers but names and faces that you knew. Life as you knew it seems like a distant memory. Who would have thought that face masks and sanitisers would be at the top of your shopping list every month?

But daughter, now is not the time to cower in fear. I know you've lost some people who were precious to you. I heard you cry out, asking Me why I healed some and not others. You have so many questions but daughter, even when you don't understand, hold on to Me. I am still God. I am still on the throne. The news and social media may say we are living in uncertain times but you serve a God who knows the end from the beginning. Nothing ever comes as a surprise to me. I am still in control. Fear not.

PSALM 91

"[5] You will not fear the terror of night, nor the arrow that flies by day, [6] nor the pestilence that stalks in the darkness, nor the plague that destroys at midday. [7] A thousand may fall at your side, ten thousand at your right hand, but it will not come near you."

Dear Father,

PSALM 91:9-10

"[9] If you say, "The LORD is my refuge," and you make the Most High your dwelling, [10] no harm will overtake you, no disaster will come near your tent."

Dear Daughter,

Breathe.

You've been so stressed lately. You job is demanding. You have deadlines to meet. You have Bible Study. Three assignments are due next week, you missed an important family dinner because you had to work late, and the washing is piling up. You are running on empty.

Daughter, you do not always have to be everything to everyone. It's okay to say no sometimes. I know you feel guilty about saying no but you do not need to save the whole world. I already did that. Come to Me and let Me fill your cup. Sit down, make yourself some tea, put on some praise and worship and just breathe.

MATTHEW 11:28-30

"[28] Come to Me, all you who labour and are heavy laden, and I will
give you rest. [29] Take My yoke upon you and learn from Me, for I
am [a]gentle and lowly in heart, and you will find rest for your souls.
30 For My yoke is easy and My burden is light."

Dear Father,

MARK 6:31

"Come with Me by yourselves to a quiet place and get some rest."

Dear Daughter,

Prepare!

Dear Father,

LUKE 14:28-30

"For which of you, desiring to build a tower, does not first sit down and count the cost, whether he has enough to complete it? Otherwise, when he has laid a foundation and is not able to finish, all who see it begin to mock him, saying, 'This man began to build and was not able to finish.'"

www.ingramcontent.com/pod-product-compliance
Lightning Source LLC
LaVergne TN
LVHW051015080826
845145LV00009B/2632

* 9 7 8 1 7 7 6 3 0 6 7 5 6 *